Eleanor Roosevelt

Karen Davila

PEARSON

Boston, Massachusetts
Chandler, Arizona
Glenview, Illinois
Upper Saddle River, New Jersey

Illustrations
6 Bradley Clark.

Photographs
Every effort has been made to secure permission and provide appropriate credit for photographic material.
The publisher deeply regrets any omission and pledges to correct errors called to its attention in subsequent editions.

Unless otherwise acknowledged, all photographs are the property of Pearson Education, Inc.

Photo locators denoted as follows: Top (T), Center (C), Bottom (B), Left (L), Right (R), Background (Bkgd)

All Photos: Courtesy of FDR Library, Hyde Park, NY.

Copyright © 2013 by Pearson Education, Inc., or its affiliates. All rights
reserved. Printed in the United States of America. This publication is protected
by copyright, and permission should be obtained from the publisher prior to
any prohibited reproduction, storage in a retrieval system, or transmission in
any form by any means, electronic, mechanical, photocopying, recording, or
likewise. For information regarding permissions, write to Pearson Curriculum
Rights & Permissions, One Lake Street, Upper Saddle River, New Jersey 07458.

Pearson® is a trademark, in the U.S. and/or in other countries,
of Pearson Inc. or its affiliates.

ISBN-13: 978-0-328-67566-1
ISBN-10:   0-328-67566-0

1 2 3 4 5 6 7 8 9 10   V0FL   15 14 13 12 11

Eleanor Roosevelt was once shy.

She changed as she grew up.

Her husband became **president**.

She was a strong **first lady**.

She spoke out for people's **rights**.

She helped people everywhere.

Glossary

first lady title for the wife of a president

president the leader of our country

rights what people should be free to do